12 REASONS TO LOVE
VOLLEYBALL

by Todd Kortemeier

STORY
LIBRARY

www.12StoryLibrary.com

12-Story Library is an imprint of Bookstaves.

Photographs ©: Jeff Roberson/AP Images, cover, 1; Monkey Business Images/Shutterstock Images, 4, 20; paulinux/Shutterstock Images, 5; Sergey Novikov/Shutterstock Images, 6; Phovoir/Shutterstock Images, 7; lazyllama/Shutterstock Images, 8; Pukhov Konstantin/Shutterstock Images, 9, 26, 29; N. Masaki/AP Images, 10; A.Ricardo/Shutterstock Images, 11; zippy/Shutterstock Images, 12, 16, 28; Petr David Josek/AP Images, 13; Michael Spomer/Cal Sport Media/AP Images, 14; Aspen Photo/Shutterstock Images, 15, 21; Kzenon/Shutterstock Images, 17; muzsy/Shutterstock, 18; Chris O'Meara/AP Images, 19; oliveromg/Shutterstock Images, 22; William Perugini/Shutterstock Images, 23; Maridav/Shutterstock Images, 24; Pal2iyawit/Shutterstock Images, 25; Iliya Pitalev/Sputnik/AP Images, 27

Library of Congress Cataloging-in-Publication Data
Names: Kortemeier, Todd, 1986- author.
Title: 12 reasons to love volleyball / by Todd Kortemeier.
Other titles: Twelve reasons to love volleyball.
Description: Mankato, Minnesota : 12-Story Library, 2018. | Series: Sports report | Includes bibliographical references and index. | Audience: Grade 4 to 6.
Identifiers: LCCN 2016047147 (print) | LCCN 2016052598 (ebook) | ISBN 9781632354327 (hardcover : alk. paper) | ISBN 9781632355010 (pbk. : alk. paper) | ISBN 9781621435532 (hosted e-book)
Subjects: LCSH: Volleyball--Juvenile literature.
Classification: LCC GV1015.34 .K67 2018 (print) | LCC GV1015.34 (ebook) | DDC 796.325--dc23
LC record available at https://lccn.loc.gov/2016047147

Printed in the United States of America
January 2019

Access free, up-to-date content on this topic plus a full digital version of this book. Scan the QR code on page 31 or use your school's login at 12StoryLibrary.com.

Table of Contents

The Serve Starts the Action

Every volleyball point starts with a serve. A good serve can make all the difference in a game.

When playing for fun, players often use an underhand serve. They hold the ball with one hand. Then they strike it from below with the other. It's easy to serve this way. But it's also easy for the other team to return this type of serve.

Top players use an overhand serve. They throw the ball into the air. Then they hit it when it's above their heads. Servers can put more power into the serve this way. That makes it harder to return.

The most exciting serve in volleyball is the jump serve. Servers start a few feet behind the court. They run

In volleyball, a serve sets the game in motion.

up, toss the ball in the air, and jump to hit it. This allows them to hit the ball downward. It comes in hard and fast at the other team. It's not easy to get underneath the ball and set it up for a return. More aces come from jump serves than any other kind. An ace is a serve that scores a point.

A jump serve can reach speeds of more than 60 miles per hour

32.8

Feet (10 m), the max height a player can toss the ball in a jump serve.

- Every volleyball point starts with a serve.
- In games for fun, an underhand serve is common.
- Top players use overhand serves, including jump serves.
- The jump serve is very fast and hard to return.

(97 km/h). At the 2016 Olympics, Ivan Zaytsev tied a record with a serve of more than 82 miles per hour (127 km/h). Zaytsev shares the Olympic record with two other players.

Volleyball Was Born in Massachusetts

In 1895, William G. Morgan led physical education at the Young Men's Christian Association (YMCA) in Holyoke, Massachusetts. YMCAs are athletic clubs. Morgan wanted to find a game that was a fun form of exercise.

Morgan's friend James Naismith worked for another YMCA in Massachusetts. In 1891, Naismith invented a new game: basketball. But Morgan knew basketball was too hard for some YMCA members.

Morgan wanted his new game to be like tennis. However, he wanted something simpler. So he kept the net but raised it above the head of the average-sized man. Next he had to find a good ball to use. A basketball didn't work. Finally, he had to have a company make one.

The first official volleyball game was played in 1896. It was held in nearby Springfield,

The game everyone loves today was first invented in 1895.

NAMING THE SPORT

When first created in 1895, volleyball was called Mintonette. That's because it was like badminton, a form of tennis with a higher net. It became known as volleyball in 1896. A volley is the flight of something in the air. Volleyball was a fitting name. Teams must volley the ball back and forth until a point is scored.

Massachusetts, the home of Naismith's basketball.

Holyoke is still considered the home of volleyball. It's also home to the International Volleyball Hall of Fame. The hall features the best players and people from the sport's history.

Volleyball was created not long after basketball was created.

78
Inches (2 m), which is the original height of the net in 1895.

- William G. Morgan invented volleyball in 1895 in Holyoke, Massachusetts.
- The first official game was played in 1896.
- Holyoke is the home of the International Volleyball Hall of Fame.

3

It's a Global Game

What started in Massachusetts has spread around the world. The Fédération Internationale de Volleyball (FIVB) oversees the sport. It began in 1947 with 14 countries. The FIVB now has 220 member countries. That makes it the largest international sports organization in the world.

The FIVB is large because volleyball is one of the five most popular sports in the world. There are 800 million people in the world who play volleyball at least once a week. That's about one in 10 people on the planet.

Volleyball is especially popular in Brazil. Before the 1980s, volleyball wasn't well known in Brazil. But all that changed in 1982. In a game leading up to the FIVB World Championship, the Brazilian men's team beat the Soviet Union. The Soviet Union was a former country that included Russia. At the time, the Soviet Union was the best volleyball team in the world. Brazil winning was a major upset. The win helped Brazilians learn about

People in Brazil enjoy a game of volleyball on the beach.

volleyball. It's now the country's second-most popular sport, behind soccer.

Russians also take volleyball very seriously. Superleague is an organization of Russian volleyball teams. It features many of the sport's biggest stars, including some Americans. Arenas are packed with fans. Similar leagues exist in Italy, Turkey, and South Korea.

In Russia, volleyball players earn large salaries.

95,887

Number of people who attended a 1983 match between Brazil and the Soviet Union.

- The Fédération Internationale de Volleyball has 220 member countries.
- It is the largest international sports organization in the world.
- Volleyball is very popular in Brazil and Russia.

THINK ABOUT IT

Why do you think volleyball is so popular around the world? How does it compare to other popular sports such as soccer?

Olympians Go for Gold

As popular as indoor volleyball is around the world, it wasn't an Olympic sport until 1964. It was first played at the Tokyo Games. Japan was a good place for Olympic volleyball to begin. The Japanese had embraced the sport early on. They were playing in 1896. That's one year after its invention in the United States.

When volleyball joined the Olympics, Japan was one of the best Olympic teams. The men's team won bronze in 1964, silver in 1968, and gold in 1972. The women's team was even better. They won two silvers and a gold between 1964 and 1972. As of 2016, Japan has won nine total medals in volleyball.

The Soviet Union has won the most medals at 12. The Soviet Union broke apart in 1991. Since then, Russia has won six medals. In 1992, the women from

Japan (white jerseys) takes on the Soviet Union at the 1964 Olympics.

12

Teams each in the men's and women's volleyball tournaments in the Olympics.

- Volleyball first joined the Olympics in 1964.
- The Soviet Union and Russia have 18 medals combined.
- Three volleyball players have each won a record four medals.

After the 2016 Olympics, three volleyball players are tied for the most medals. They have each won four. Inna Ryskal played for the Soviet Union. Sergey Tetyukhin played for Russia. And Samuele Papi played for Italy. Ryskal is also the only volleyball player to have won two gold medals.

the former Soviet Union played as the Unified Team. They also won a medal.

Other countries have been successful in the Olympics, too. Brazil has 10 medals. So does the United States. From 1992 to 2000, Cuba won three golds in the women's tournament.

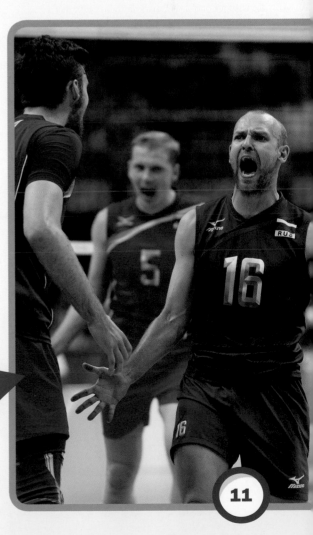

Players from Team Russia celebrate on the court.

Beach Volleyball Takes It to the Sand

Players hit a ball over a net in beach volleyball. But that's about all it has in common with indoor volleyball. In many ways, beach volleyball is a different sport.

Beach volleyball is played with just two players per team. There are no substitutions. That means the same two players play the entire game. Players can also move anywhere on the court. They can even hit the ball from the other team's side. These rules make the beach game very exciting.

Where the first beach volleyball game was played isn't clear. Some people say it was in Hawaii. Others say it may have been in Santa Monica, California. The first two-man beach volleyball game was in Santa Monica in 1930.

Beach volleyball became an Olympic sport in 1996. It has been very popular since then. From 2004 to 2012, Americans Misty May-Treanor and Kerri Walsh Jennings dominated the women's competition. They won three gold medals in a row.

Beach volleyball players must move fast to cover the entire court.

After May-Treanor retired, Walsh Jennings won bronze with partner April Ross in 2016. Walsh Jennings is considered the best beach volleyball player ever.

Kerri Walsh Jennings has a record four medals in beach volleyball.

2016

Year beach volleyball first appeared as a National Collegiate Athletic Association sport.

- Beach volleyball is different from indoor volleyball.
- Beach volleyball is one of the most popular Olympic sports.
- Kerri Walsh Jennings has the most Olympic beach volleyball medals.

The Libero Plays a Special Role

Nearly 100 years after volleyball was invented, an important rule was added. Since the beginning, players could be hitters, blockers, or setters. But then, in 1998, a new position was introduced for indoor volleyball. It's called the libero. Liberos first appeared at the 1998 World Championships. The position makes the game more exciting.

The word *libero* means "free" in Italian. It's a good name for the position. Liberos are free to play anywhere in the back row. Liberos also never need to come out of the game. Other players must rotate out at certain times. This is called substitution.

A libero moves fast to get under the ball.

However, liberos are not free in other ways. Liberos cannot block shots. They also can't make attack shots. Those are shots aimed at the opponent's side.

Liberos play a special role for defense. They often save their teams by keeping the ball in play. Many times they get down on their knees or dive for spikes. They may have the toughest position in the sport.

Because of their special roles, liberos wear special jerseys. It's a different color than the team's main jersey.

2
Number of liberos allowed per team for international matches.

- The libero position was created in 1998.
- The libero is a special player for defense.
- Liberos wear different jerseys than the rest of the team.

OTHER VOLLEYBALL POSITIONS

All positions play special roles in volleyball. Hitters usually play near the net. They make powerful shots. Blockers stop shots from getting over the net. And setters set the ball up for hitters. Teams may make three plays before the ball goes over the net. These are often a dig, a set, and a hit.

Digs Can Save a Team

Liberos are known for their digs against spikes. Spikes come in fast. A spike is a shot hit downward at the floor. It often scores a point. To keep the play alive, a team has to act fast to return a spike. That's where a dig comes in. A dig can save the day.

To dig, players must judge the speed of the ball. They should be ready to move in any direction. They must get a part of their body to the ball somehow.

Whenever possible, players want to dig with both forearms. It's easier to control the ball that way. It's more likely to fly up when using two hands. But sometimes players can dig only with one hand. In that case, it's best to use a fist.

Other times a player must dive to make a dig. A dive might be the hardest dig to make. A lot happens in a dive. Players first must get down

A forearm dig.

Landing in sand isn't as bad as landing on a gym floor.

low. Then they must make good contact with the ball. Last, they have to try hitting it in the right direction. And all that is done while flying through the air. Diving on sand isn't too hard. But it's not so easy on a hard court. That makes for a tough landing.

THINK ABOUT IT

Imagine a spike is coming in. You have to dive to dig it. What would be going through your mind? How would you feel if you missed it?

50

College volleyball record for digs by one player in a three-set match.

- A dig helps keep the ball alive for a team.
- Making contact with both forearms helps make a good dig.
- Sometimes players must dive to dig.

17

Being Tall Helps

In men's volleyball, the net is nearly eight feet (2.43 m) high. It's eight inches (20.3 cm) shorter for women. It's not surprising that most volleyball players are taller than average.

On the 2016 US men's Olympic team, nearly every player was six feet three (1.9 m) or taller. Many were six feet eight (2.0 m) or taller. Taller players can get their arms above the net to block or spike.

Russians Dmitriy Muserskiy and Aleksey Kazakov are two of the tallest volleyball players ever.

Tall players play up front, where they can spike.

SHORTER OLYMPIANS

Being tall is helpful in volleyball. But there are many examples of shorter Olympic players. At five feet eleven (1.8 m), Eric Sato was a key part of the 1988 US team that won gold. His sister, Liane Sato, played for the women's team the same year. She is only five feet four (1.6 m).

6 feet 4

Height (1.9 m) of Karsta Lowe, tallest player on the 2016 US Olympic women's volleyball team.

- Most volleyball players are taller than average.
- People of all heights can play volleyball in the proper positions.
- Shorter players make good setters or liberos.

Muserskiy stands seven feet two (2.18 m). Kazakov is seven feet one (2.16 m). Both have played at the Olympics. But an even taller player is out there. Wuttichai Suksara of Thailand is just over seven feet three (2.22 m).

Even in top levels, people of nearly any height can play volleyball. The key is to put the right players in the right places. Shorter players can pass the ball up so taller players can spike it. Shorter players also make good liberos. It can be easier to dig when a player is lower to the ground.

Dmitriy Muserskiy (left) towers over other players.

Communication Is the Key to Teamwork

Teamwork is important in all team sports. That includes volleyball. In volleyball, most players come in and out of the game many times. No matter which players are in, the team needs to work together. This is true at the Olympic level, at the youth league level, and every level in between.

Communication is a big part of teamwork. To communicate means to share information. Players can communicate with their voices or with signals. It helps all parts of the game.

Volleyball teammates learn to rely on each other.

A player gives his team hand signals before a play.

Before the match, players should watch the other team warming up. They might notice something useful to share. That's a helpful form of communication.

Before the serve, each player needs to be in the right place. They need to communicate about the area they'll each cover. Things happen fast when the ball is coming over the net. It's important to share information about who will hit the ball. That's known as calling for the ball. If no one calls for the ball, the team won't know what to do. Maybe no one will go for the ball. It might fall to the ground.

12
Number of substitutions a team can have per set in international play.

- Teamwork is important in volleyball.
- Communication is a big part of teamwork.
- Players communicate out loud and with hand signals.

Not all communication in volleyball is spoken out loud. Sometimes players need to share information the other team shouldn't hear. In these situations, players use hand signals. For example, maybe a team wants to try scoring on their opponent's right corner. A player will put one finger behind his or her back. That tells the server where to aim the serve.

Volleyball Is a Great Workout

Volleyball is popular worldwide for many reasons. People love it because it's fun and exciting. People also love it because it's healthy for the body and mind.

Playing volleyball is great exercise. It burns fat and calories. Different players burn calories in different ways. It depends on the players' sizes and how they play. People playing for fun don't burn as many calories as people playing in more serious games. And people playing on sand burn more than people in a gym. That's because it's harder to move on sand. In any case, burning calories helps people keep their bodies strong and healthy.

With fast action, volleyball is a fun workout.

Volleyball works many muscles in the body. It especially helps the arms, legs, and chest. But playing builds more than just strong muscles. It also builds quick muscles and improves balance. The heart and lungs get a workout as well.

Volleyball is good for the brain, too. Playing helps hand-eye coordination. That's when the brain and hands must work together to make a play. Volleyball helps

> Volleyball requires a lot of focus.

players focus and concentrate. Volleyball also improves mood.

Working with teammates is another way volleyball helps the brain. Players learn how to communicate with others. They learn to be good leaders as well.

20

Minutes of volleyball it takes to equal the energy spent jogging one mile.

- Volleyball is a fun way to exercise.
- The sport strengthens muscles.
- It also exercises the brain.

INJURY RISKS

Playing volleyball carries a few health risks. It's a jumping sport. That means leg injuries can be common. It can be hard on the knees. Ankles can twist. Many players wear braces to help these parts. Proper training can help prevent injuries, too.

The Sport Has Many Variations

Volleyball is a very simple sport. All it takes is a net and a ball. But some people don't have enough space or players for a full game. That's why there are many ways to play the sport.

Hoover-Ball takes volleyball to the next level. A volleyball weighs a little more than nine ounces (260 g). But Hoover-Ball uses a medicine ball weighing four to six pounds (1.8 to 2.7 kg). Players catch and throw the ball over the net. It was invented in 1928 as exercise for President Herbert Hoover.

Blind volleyball adds surprise. A sheet or tarp covers the net to the floor. Players can't see the other team. All they see is the ball coming over. Players must move quickly.

In Hoover–Ball, the weight of the medicine ball builds strong muscles.

75

Miles per hour (120 km/h) the Sunback Spike kick can reach in Sepak Takraw.

- Volleyball has many variations.
- Hoover-Ball uses a heavy ball.
- Wallyball is played on a racquetball court.
- Sepak Takraw is an ancient game from Asia.

Wallyball is a smaller form of volleyball. It's played on a racquetball court. There are two to four players per team.

Sepak Takraw is full of wild action.

THINK ABOUT IT

Can you think of a new way to play volleyball? What other sports could you combine with it?

The walls of the court are in play. That means players can bounce shots off the walls. These can be very hard to return.

Sepak Takraw is much older than volleyball. It was invented in Southeast Asia in the 1000s. The court is like a volleyball court. But players cannot use their arms or hands to return the ball. They must use their legs, head, or chest. Players fly through the air with kicks.

Sitting Volleyball Allows All to Play

Sitting volleyball is another version of volleyball. It's an adapted sport. That means the rules have been adjusted so people with disabilities can play.

Sitting volleyball was invented in the Netherlands in 1956. It was based on a German sport called Sitzball. Sitzball was played while seated but with no net.

A sitting volleyball court is smaller than a volleyball court. It is 32.8 feet (10 m) by 19.7 feet (6 m). The net is placed just a few feet off the ground. Players must have some part of their upper body touching the floor when they hit the ball. Most other rules are the same. Teams can make three hits before the ball goes over the net.

The sport is very competitive. It has many of the same exciting

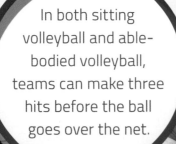

In both sitting volleyball and able-bodied volleyball, teams can make three hits before the ball goes over the net.

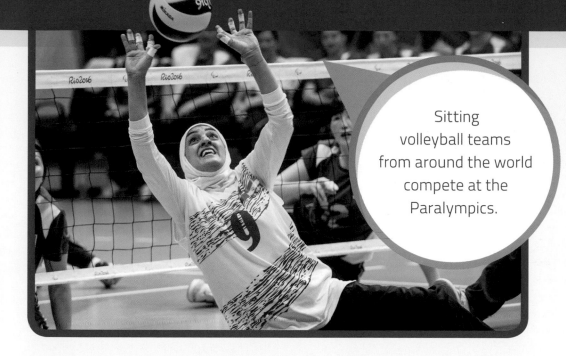

Sitting volleyball teams from around the world compete at the Paralympics.

moments as volleyball. Players must move fast when someone spikes the ball.

Men's sitting volleyball joined the Paralympics in 1980. The

Paralympics are the Olympic Games for people with disabilities. Women's sitting volleyball was added in 2004.

Iran has been one of the best teams in men's sitting volleyball. They have won seven Paralympic medals. The United States and China have been the best in the women's tournament. They each have three medals.

Standing volleyball was once a Paralympic sport as well. It's for players who can stand but have disabilities that make it difficult to move. It was last played at the Paralympics in 2000.

187
Number of sitting volleyball players who competed at the 2016 Paralympics.

- Sitting volleyball was invented in 1956.
- It joined the Paralympics in 1980 for men and 2004 for women.
- The court is smaller, and the net is low to the ground.

Fact Sheet

- Indoor volleyball matches last for a maximum of five sets. In the first four sets, a team must score at least 25 points to win. In the last set, the winner must score at least 15 points. A team must win by two points to take a set.

- In 1998, there was a big change in how the game is scored. Before, a team needed to be serving to score. The winning team needed only 15 points per set. But now either team can score whether they served or not. This is called the rally scoring system. When the receiving team scores, they also win back the serve.

- A volleyball team has six players on the court. Every time a team wins back a serve, one player must change position. The exception to this rule is the libero. The libero can play anywhere in the back row.

- High school and lower-level volleyball competitions usually play on a gym floor. The Olympics are played on a special surface called Taraflex. This layered surface is very smooth and strong. It has been used at every Olympics since 1976. Some school gyms use it as well.

- An indoor volleyball court requires a lot of space above the net. The minimum roof height is 23 feet (7 m).

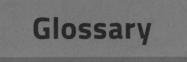

Glossary

ace
When a team's serve is not returned.

calories
Units of energy found in food.

defense
In sports, an action meant to protect a team or prevent the other team from scoring.

hand-eye coordination
Using visual information to help guide the hand to complete a task, such as hitting a ball.

overhand
A throwing motion in which the hand is raised above the shoulder.

racquetball
A sport played on a walled court in which players hit shots with a racquet.

spike
In volleyball, a fast-moving return shot hit directly toward the floor on the opponent's side.

substitution
Replacing one player from a game with another.

underhand
A throwing motion in which the hand never rises above the shoulder.

upset
When a supposedly weaker team beats a stronger team.

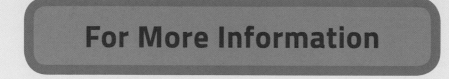

Books

Abramovitz, Melissa. *Volleyball*. Detroit, MI: Lucent, 2013.

Doeden, Matt. *Volleyball*. Mankato, MN: Amicus High Interest, 2016.

Schwartz, Heather E. *Top Volleyball Tips*. Mankato, MN: Capstone, 2017.

Visit 12StoryLibrary.com

Scan the code or use your school's login at **12StoryLibrary.com** for recent updates about this topic and a full digital version of this book. Enjoy free access to:

- Digital ebook
- Breaking news updates
- Live content feeds
- Videos, interactive maps, and graphics
- Additional web resources

Note to educators: Visit 12StoryLibrary.com/register to sign up for free premium website access. Enjoy live content plus a full digital version of every 12-Story Library book you own for every student at your school.

Index

About the Author

Todd Kortemeier is a journalist and children's author from Minnesota. He has written more than 50 books for young people, primarily on sports topics. He and his wife live in Minneapolis.